I CAN DO THAT!
Creative play for can-do kids

STICKER HERO

How to Use This Book

Most of the activities in this book are easy enough for your child to complete without help, but you should provide instructions. Some challenges include extra stickers that your child can place anywhere they wish.

Build Skills While Playing

Playing with stickers is a marvelous way to hone fine motor skills, hand-eye coordination, and spatial relations. Your child will use stickers to solve mazes, play matching and counting games, and decorate pictures. At the same time, they will:

- practice skills such as decision making and thinking ahead

- enhance the ability to sort and match objects by size, shape, and color

- develop observation skills

- strengthen counting skills

- build confidence

- increase vocabulary

- exercise creativity

Play Together!

Studies show that children learn best when they are engaged with an adult. Stimulate conversation by asking your child to point to and name the animals, objects, colors, or shapes on the page. More important, create meaningful experiences for your child as they learn through play!

MAKE PAIRS OF SOCKS

The bears hung their socks out to dry.
Put the matching sticker next to each sock to make pairs.

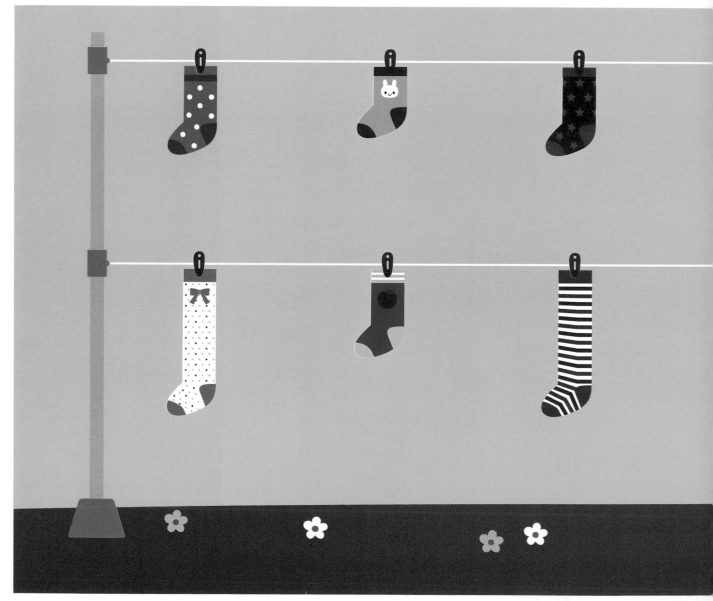

HOME SWEET HOME

The animals want to go to their homes. Follow the paths to help each animal get home.
Then put each animal's sticker in its house.

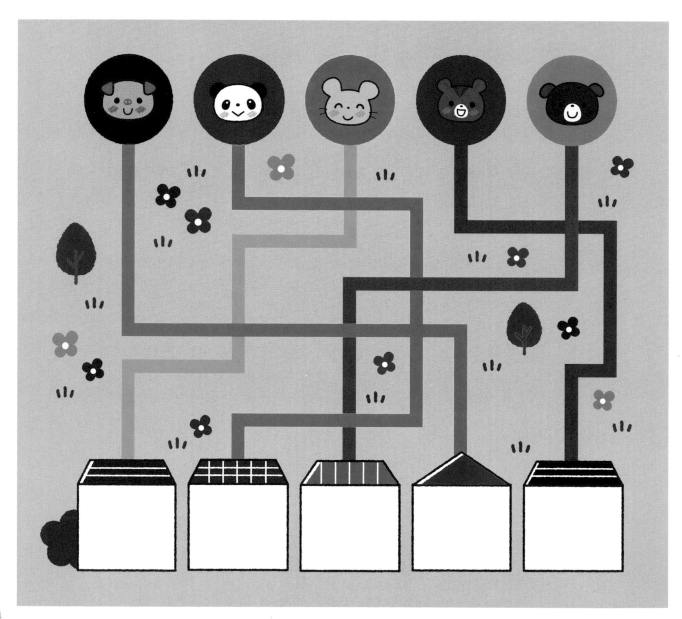

MATCHING SHOES

Put the matching sticker next to each shoe to make pairs.

AT THE BAKERY

These friends are ready for dessert.
Use stickers to put different desserts on each plate.

ANIMAL MATCH

What animals will these friends see on their walk? Go through the path from ➡ to ➡. Then put each animal sticker on its matching shadow to complete the picture.

IN THE SEA

Who lives in the sea? Put stickers on each ● to complete the sea animals.
Then add some bubbles!

BEAR PUZZLE

Go through the path from ➡ to ➡ following only 🐻.
As you go, put stickers on the bears you've passed.

APPLE MAZE

Follow the path from ➡ to ➡. Always go in the direction of the larger number.
When you're done, add stickers so the number of apples matches the number on the path.

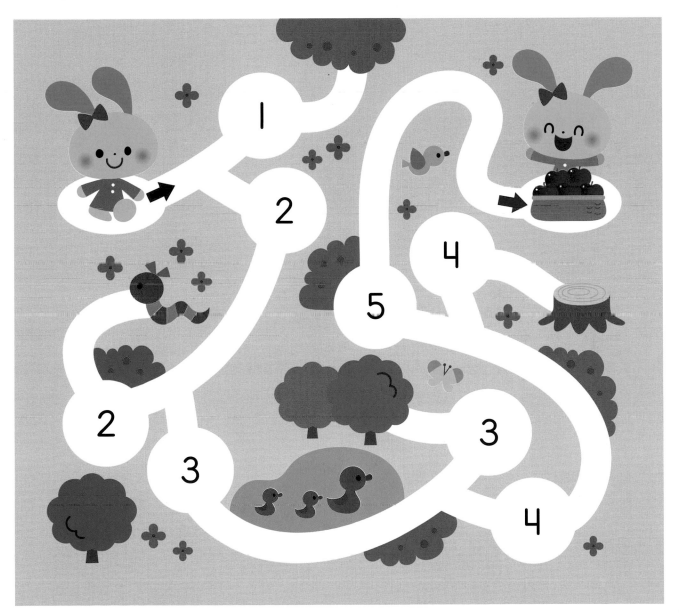

A TRIP TO SQUIRREL'S HOUSE

Place a sticker on the ▮ with the matching ★. Then follow the path from ➡ to ➡. Use stickers to add decorations!

ON THE JOB

Put stickers next to each animal so the objects match their job.

AT THE SUPERMARKET

Put vegetable stickers in the yellow cart so it matches the shopping list.

WHAT IS MISSING?

Add school supply stickers to the box on the right so it matches the box on the left.

COOKIE MATCH

Add cookie stickers to each plate until they all match the example.

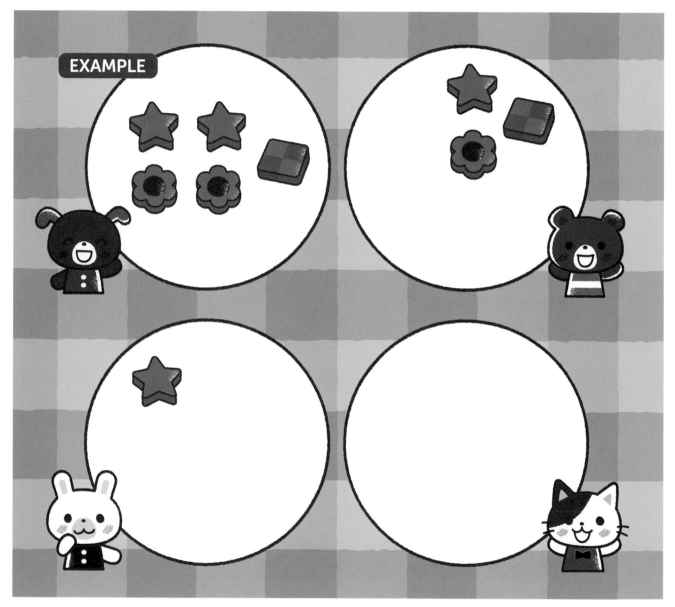

LET'S MAKE FLOWERS BLOOM

Follow the path from ➡ to ➡. As you go, place stickers on the flowers to make them bloom. Remember, you can only follow the same path once. Add more stickers to the garden!

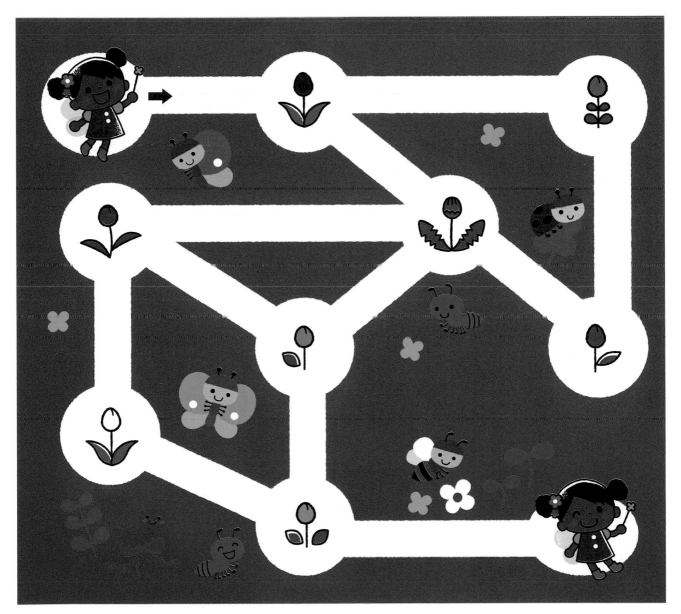

CAT CHASE

The cat ran away with the little girl's fish! Help her collect them. Follow the path of the fish to reach the cat. As you go, put paw print stickers on the rooms you passed.

SEA CREATURES

What sea creatures do you see? Follow the path from ➡ to ➡, and place each sticker on its matching shadow.

AIRPLANE MAZE

Place a sticker on the ⬜ with the matching ★. Then follow the path in the airplane from ➡ to ➡. When you're done, add more flying machines and clouds to the sky!

MATCH THE NUMBERS

Count the number of items in each box and place stickers on their matching shadows. Then count the items in the first row and add that number sticker to the ▪.

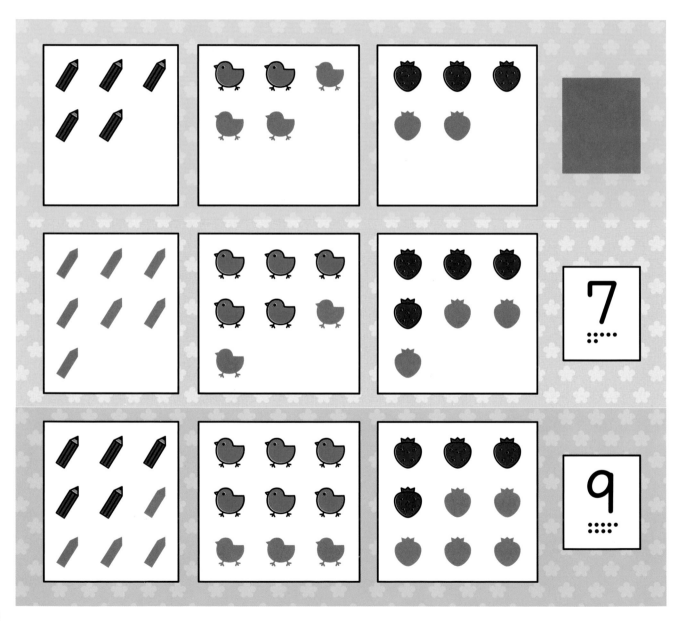

PLAYGROUND GAMES

It's time to play in the park! Go through the maze from ➡ to ➡.
As you go, place each playground sticker on its matching shadow.

JEWELRY BOX

There are three different kinds of rings in the box. Count each kind and put that number of stickers in the ☐. Which one has the smallest number? Put that sticker in the ☐.

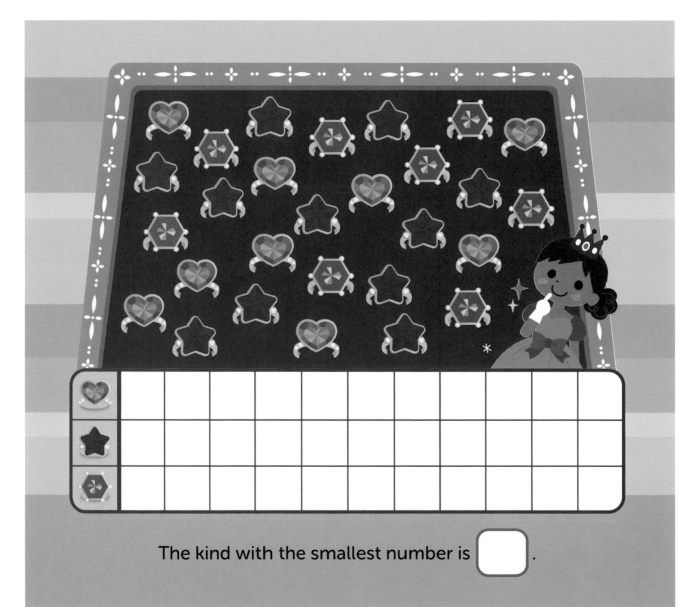

The kind with the smallest number is ☐ .

LET'S COUNT TO 12!

Count the items in each box. Then add that number sticker to the ▪.

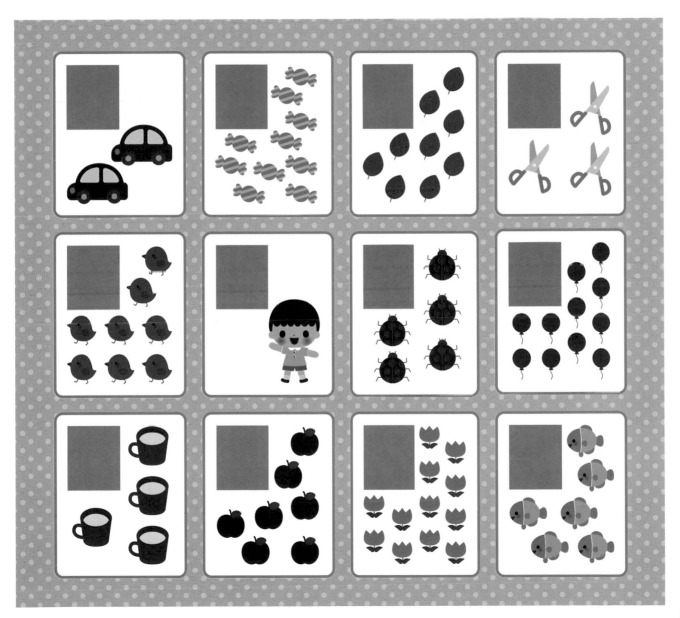

LET'S HAND OUT BALLOONS

Follow the path from ➡ to ➡. As you go, use stickers to give each animal a balloon!
Remember, you can only follow the same path once. Add more fun stickers to the park.

ABC MAZE

Follow the path in order of the alphabet. As you go, put stickers on the path so the first letter of the picture matches the letter in the circle.

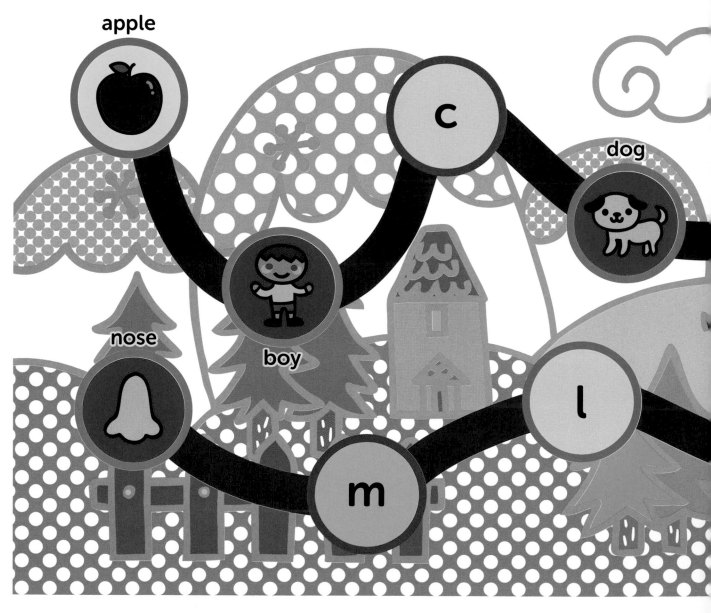

apple

c

dog

nose

boy

l

m

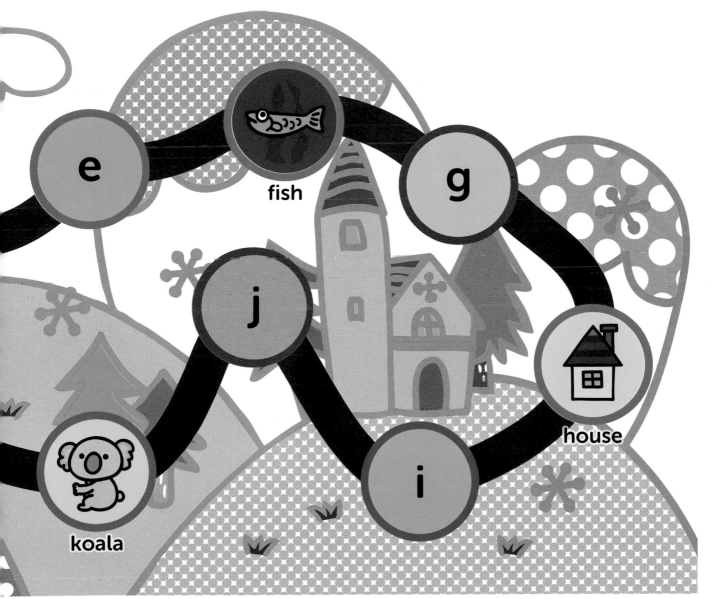

e

fish

g

j

koala

i

house

33

TIME FOR TREATS

Follow the path from ➡ to ➡. Then place stickers in this order: 🧁 🍰 🍩 🫐.

PUT NUMBERS IN ORDER

Add stickers to the remote control, clock, and telephone so the numbers are in the correct order.

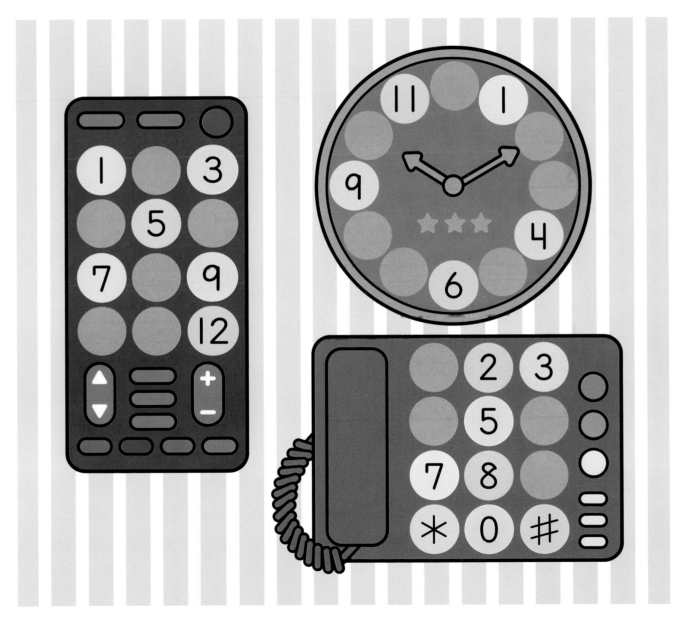

LET'S FIX THE BRIDGES

Use stickers to fix the broken bridges. Then follow the path from ➡ to ➡.

SCOOPS OF ICE CREAM

How many scoops of ice cream did each person order? Place stickers on each cone to match the number of ice cream scoops each person ordered.

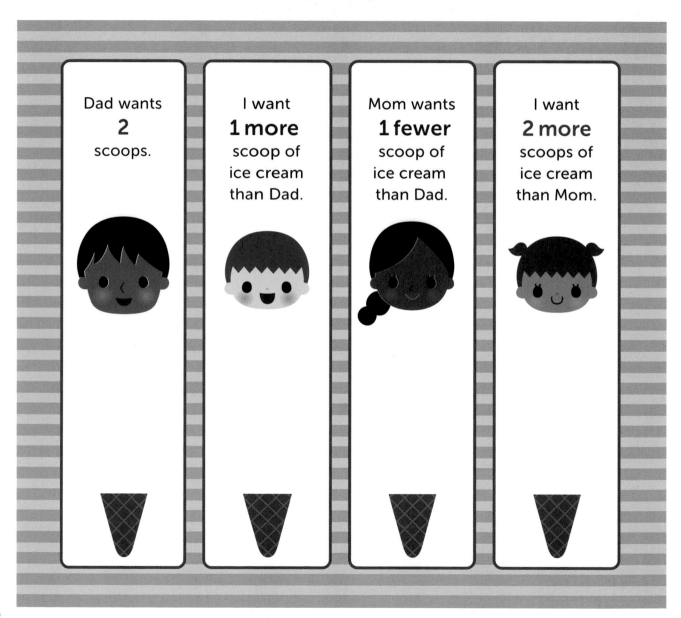

Dad wants **2** scoops.

I want **1 more** scoop of ice cream than Dad.

Mom wants **1 fewer** scoop of ice cream than Dad.

I want **2 more** scoops of ice cream than Mom.

TRAIN MATCH

Each picture shows a train from the side.
Next to it, put the sticker that shows the same train from the front.

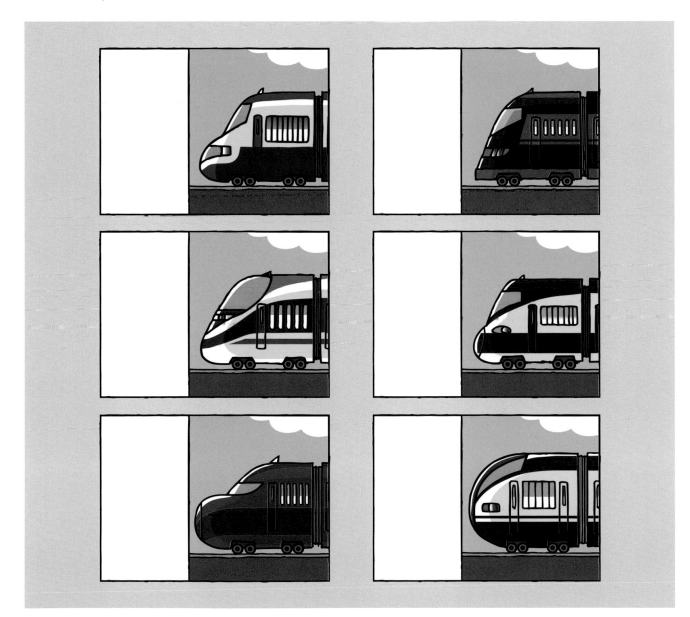

PARTY TIME!

Look at the number under each item of food. Then add that many stickers to each plate.

ANIMAL MATCH

These baby animals are looking for their mothers.
Put each mother sticker next to her baby.

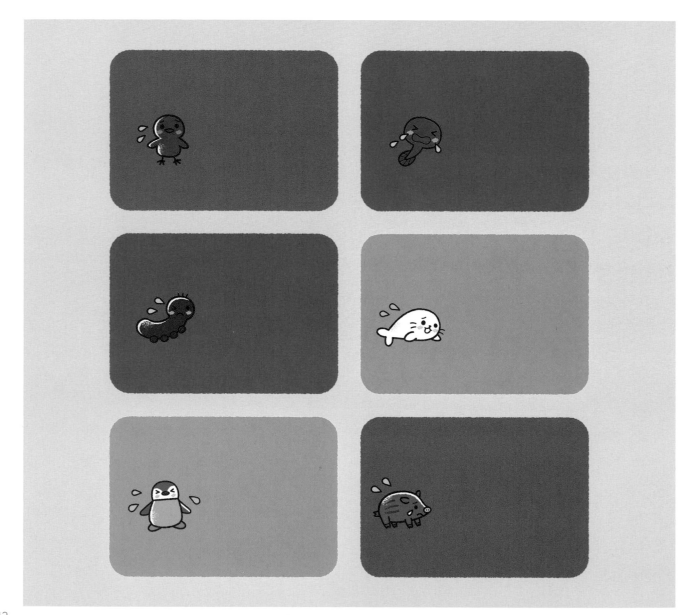

CAT ROOM

There are three different kinds of cats in the room. Count each kind and put that number of stickers in the ☐. Which kind has the largest number? Put that cat sticker in the ☐.

The kind with the largest number is ☐.

MATCHING FISH

Add fish stickers to the empty tank until it matches the full tank on the right. Then add some decorations!

ICE CREAM PARTY!

Match the number on each ice cream sundae sticker with the number on its shadow so the sundae looks like the example.

EXAMPLE

CLOUD MAZE

Help the airplane fly through the cloud to get to the sunny sky. Place a sticker on the ▓ with the matching ★. Then follow the path in the cloud from ➡ to ➡.

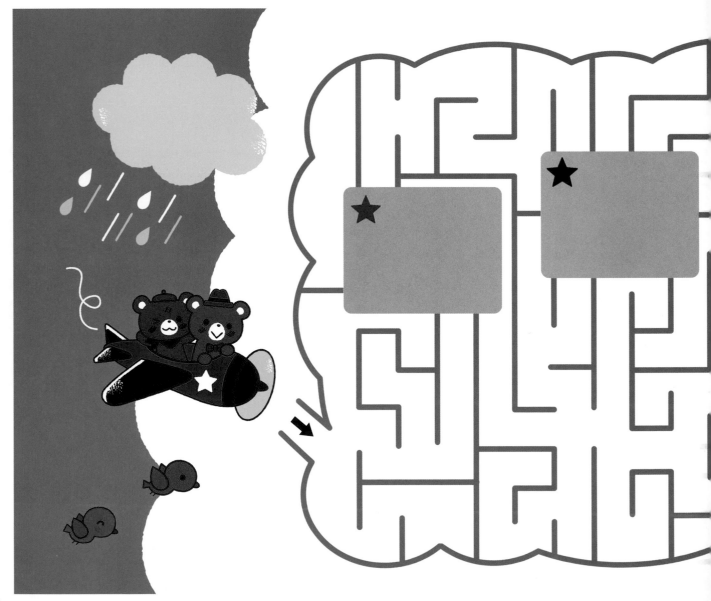

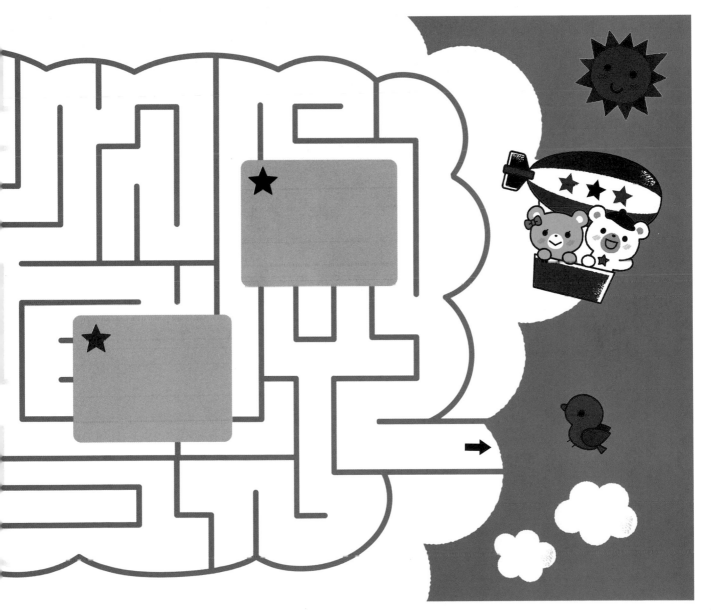

LET'S MAKE A CALENDAR

Place the number stickers in order on the calendar.
Then write the name of a month it could be in the white space.

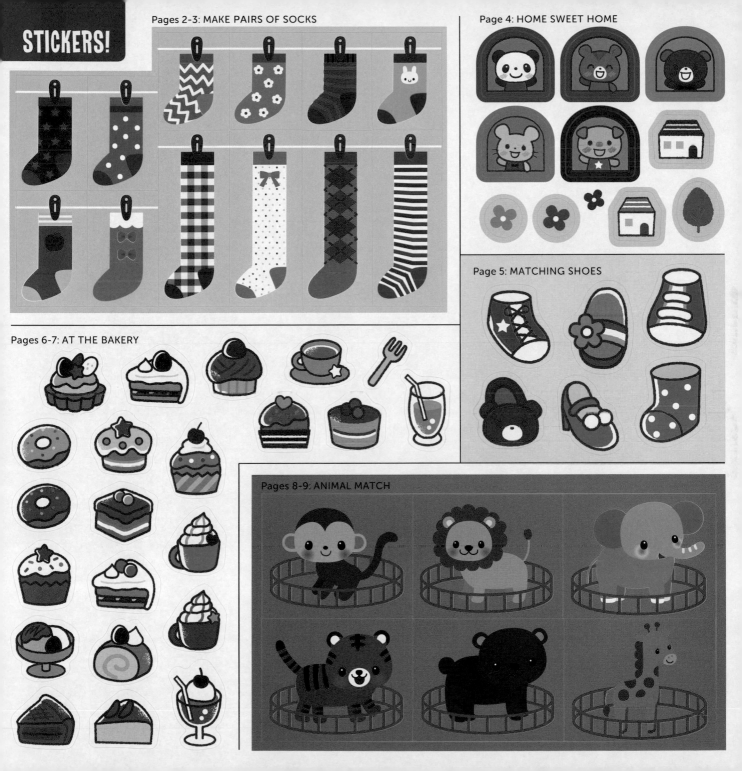

STICKERS!

Pages 2-3: MAKE PAIRS OF SOCKS

Page 4: HOME SWEET HOME

Page 5: MATCHING SHOES

Pages 6-7: AT THE BAKERY

Pages 8-9: ANIMAL MATCH

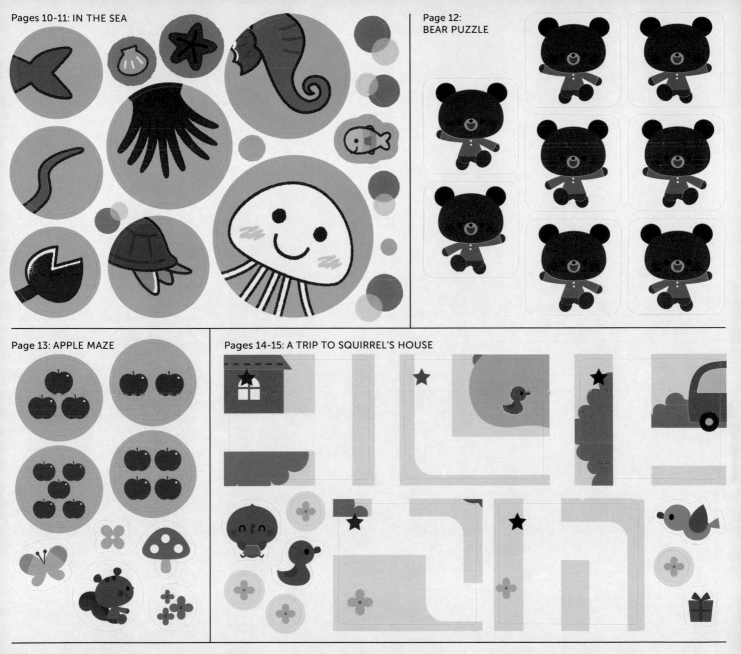

Pages 10-11: IN THE SEA

Page 12: BEAR PUZZLE

Page 13: APPLE MAZE

Pages 14-15: A TRIP TO SQUIRREL'S HOUSE

Page 16: ON THE JOB

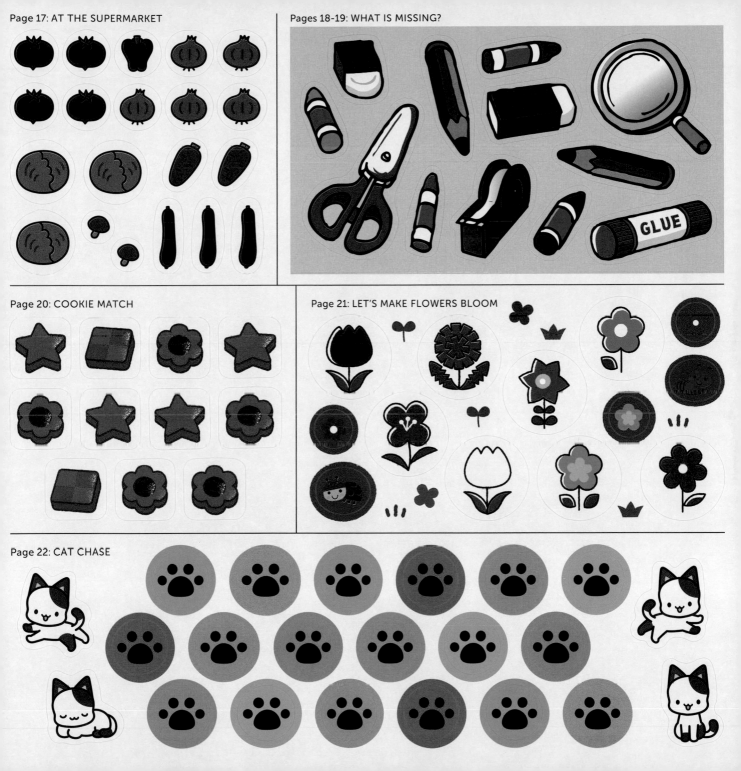

Page 17: AT THE SUPERMARKET

Pages 18-19: WHAT IS MISSING?

GLUE

Page 20: COOKIE MATCH

Page 21: LET'S MAKE FLOWERS BLOOM

Page 22: CAT CHASE

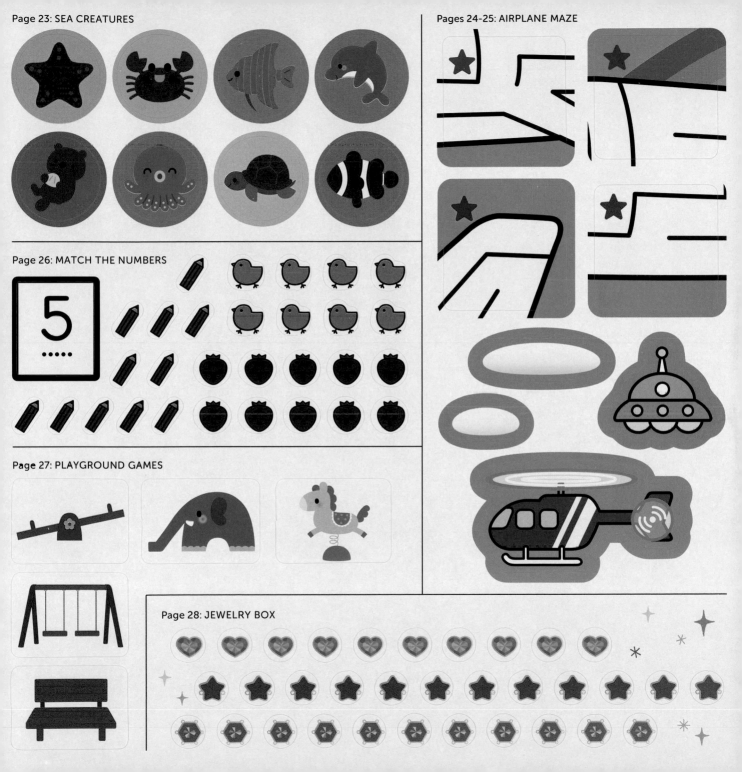

Page 23: SEA CREATURES

Pages 24-25: AIRPLANE MAZE

Page 26: MATCH THE NUMBERS

5

Page 27: PLAYGROUND GAMES

Page 28: JEWELRY BOX

Page 29: LET'S COUNT TO 12!

1   2   3

4   5   6

7   8   9

10   11   12

Pages 30-31: LET'S HAND OUT BALLOONS

Pages 32-33: ABC MAZE

Page 34: TIME FOR TREATS

Page 35: PUT NUMBERS IN ORDER

1   2   4   5

6   8   9   10   12

2   3   4   6   7   8   10   11

Pages 36-37: LET'S FIX THE BRIDGES

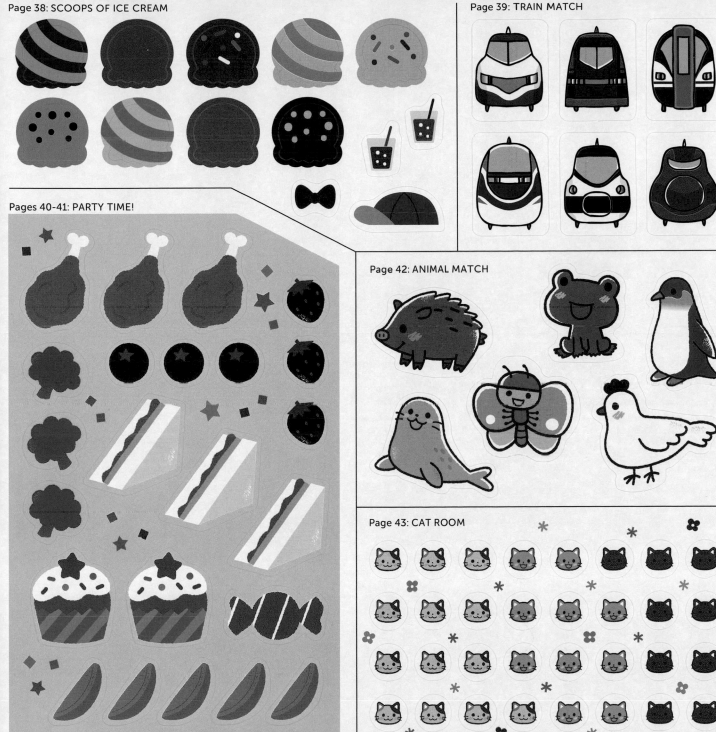

Page 38: SCOOPS OF ICE CREAM

Page 39: TRAIN MATCH

Pages 40-41: PARTY TIME!

Page 42: ANIMAL MATCH

Page 43: CAT ROOM